Published by Creative Education
P.O. Box 227, Mankato, Minnesota 56002

Creative Education is an imprint of The Creative Company.
Design by Stephanie Blumenthal
Production design by The Design Lab
Art direction by Rita Marshall
Printed in the United States of America

Photographs by Alamy Images (The Print Collector; Visual Arts Library); Corbis
(Robbie Jack); Getty Images (Louis Gabriel Blanchet; Hulton Archive; Imagno;
Imagno/Austrian Archives; Henry Nelson O'Neil; Peter Anton Lorenzoni;
Vincente de Paredes; Jacques Philippe Joseph de Saint-Quentin; Ignaz
Unterberger); The Granger Collection, New York

# WOLFGANG AMADEUS

"Letter to the Abbe Bullinger, Salzburg; Paris, 7 August 1778" (pages 42–43),
"Letter to his Father; Vienna, 15 December 1781" (pages 43–44), and "Letter to
his sister, Nannerl; Vienna, 20 April 1782" (pages 44–45) from *Mozart's Letters*,
edited by Eric Blom, translated by Emily Anderson, 1961. Reproduced by
permission of Palgrave MacMillan.

Library of Congress Cataloging-in-Publication Data

Riggs, Kate.
Wolfgang Amadeus Mozart / by Kate Riggs.
p. cm. — (Xtraordinary artists)
Includes index.
ISBN 978-1-58341-664-8
1. Mozart, Wolfgang Amadeus, 1756–1791—Juvenile literature. 2. Composers—
Austria—Biography—Juvenile literature. I. Title. II. Series.

ML3930.M9R54 2008
780'.92—dc22 [B]                    2007008963

First edition

2 4 6 8 9 7 5 3 1

# A ORDINARY ARTISTS

# MOZART

## KATE RIGGS

CREATIVE 🍎 EDUCATION

From his position at the keyboard, the young conductor waved his small hand in the air, as if coaxing the music out of the orchestra before him. With each jerk of his head, his powdered wig moved slightly, but he did not notice. All that mattered was the music—his music. Wolfgang Amadeus Mozart was a conductor, composer, and instrumentalist whose various skills failed to garner him the fame he deserved while alive. Regardless of public opinion, he knew he was doing important work. "I pay no attention whatever to anybody's praise or blame," he said. "I simply follow my own feelings." Those feelings would lead him to create music that was uniquely Mozart—music that would last forever.

On January 17, 1756, in Salzburg, Austria (which was then a part of Germany), Wolfgang Amadeus Mozart was born. To his family, young Wolfgang was known simply as "Wolferl," and he was the last of seven children born to Leopold and Anna Maria Mozart. He was only the second to survive past infancy, however, arriving five years after his older sister Maria Anna, or "Nannerl."

The year Wolfgang was born, Leopold was serving as a court composer and violinist in the orchestra of the local archbishop, the head of both the Catholic Church and the government in Salzburg. That year, Leopold published his *Essay on a Fundamental Violin Method*, which became the most widely read manual on violin playing in the last half of the 18th century. Due to his position within the community and special status as a respected

*Mozart's mother Anna Maria came from a modest Salzburg family and was known for her cheerfulness, good temper, and thrifty housekeeping*

5

A 19th-century engraving depicts what a toddler-aged Mozart might have looked like trying to play the tall-legged clavier without using a bench

musician, Leopold was able to adequately provide for his family and associate with the upper classes, but the Mozarts were not wealthy. Leopold was also able to spend much of his time at home, in a loving, highly disciplined, and instructive environment in which he schooled his children in music and academics.

Wolfgang not only looked like a Mozart—exhibiting the broad forehead, large blue-gray eyes, and fine blond hair characteristic of the family—but he also had the interests and talents of one. Even as a toddler, Wolfgang was attracted to the sound of a violin and the touch of a clavier's keyboard. When Leopold began teaching Nannerl how to play the

Starting in 1762, Leopold and the children often performed together, with Leopold playing violin, Nannerl singing, and Mozart at the clavier

7

"Young Mozart is certainly a prodigy for his age and I am really extremely fond of him.... I have so good an opinion of the innate goodness of the young man that I hope that, despite the adulation of his father, he will not allow himself to be spoilt but will turn out an honorable man."

— Italian poet Metastasio, upon meeting Mozart in 1771

*Mozart and his sister enjoyed playing duets together, especially in front of important audiences such as the Viennese court of the empress and emperor*

clavier, the three-year-old Wolfgang quietly observed her lessons, putting aside his toys and checking his rambunctious behavior. He was fascinated by the instrument and wanted to learn everything about it. He was so intent on doing just that that his father began teaching the persistent boy how to play the following year. Leopold quickly discovered that Wolfgang was a natural musician; Wolfgang learned to play each note with ease and never complained about having to practice. Nannerl was likewise impressed by her younger brother's rapid advancement and noted that he could master whatever piece their father assigned "fault-lessly, with utmost neatness, and in exact time." She encouraged him, and the two were

soon playing duets at the clavier, sitting side by side as equals.

By the time he was five, Wolfgang realized that there was more to making music than simply playing the notes that were written on the page by someone else. He wanted to write his own. He started by improvising at the clavier, creating something new out of a piece or an exercise that he had already learned. Then, he attempted to write out the music that he could hear building inside his head. As the child showed his father the smudge of notes amongst various blots of ink that was his first composition, Leopold remarked that the piece looked too difficult for anyone to play. The boy explained, "That's why it's a concerto: you

must practice it until you get it right; look, here's how it goes." And he proceeded to plunk out just enough notes so that his astonished father could understand. After that first scribbled attempt by Wolfgang, Leopold began notating his son's compositions in Nannerl's lesson notebook when the boy was six. The earliest surviving record is called "Andante for piano (K. Ia) in C"; it is dated 1761 and contains only six short measures, or bars of music.

Wolfgang began his storied career as a composer by imitating the exercises that his father wrote for the children's lessons. He soon figured out how to replicate the same forms

One of Mozart's earliest manuscripts, 1762's "Minuet in G Major" (K. 1) was once thought to have been the first piece of music Mozart wrote

and follow the same rules inherent in each composition, quickly mastering the syntax and grammar of this unique "language." The six-year-old was not daunted by the task and, curiously, was not easily frustrated by the careful process of arranging notes together to form musical phrases. For this young composer did not make many mistakes. He knew what he needed to do to structure a piece of music so that other people would be able to study it as well. Leopold was convinced that his son was a miracle, a gift from God. He was equally certain that it was his duty to let the world know about it.

In 1762, Leopold took Wolfgang and Nannerl to the capital city of Vienna, where the children played for Empress Maria Theresa and Emperor Francis I, rulers of the sprawling Austrian Habsburg Empire. Wolfgang was widely adored, not only for his surprising facility at the keyboard, but also for his charmingly childish behavior. He did not hesitate to climb onto the empress's lap or to run through the halls of the palace, chasing after the young princesses. Whenever he sat down at the clavier, though, Wolfgang was all business. "Everyone is amazed, especially at the boy," wrote Leopold to a friend back home in Salzburg. "Everyone whom I have heard says that his genius is incomprehensible."

Having made such a favorable impression on the German court, Leopold set his sights on Paris, France. Mid-18th-century Paris was the cultural center of Europe, and the court of King Louis XV was receptive to gifted musicians. Leopold believed that achieving success in Paris was the key to establishing a lasting reputation for Wolfgang, whose skill was already eclipsing his sister's and whose status as a child genius could be used for monetary gain. The family depended on subscription concerts and royal favors for the bulk of their income, and Wolfgang was the one who drew in the crowds and captivated their patrons.

After the family departed Paris, Wolfgang won over King George III and Queen Charlotte of England. In London, the precocious eight-year-old began writing symphonies, more complicated works that used many instruments, instead of the solo sonatas he was

accustomed to. The standard orchestra in Wolfgang's day included string instruments (violins, violas, cellos, and double basses), two oboes, two french horns, trumpets, and drums, with the occasional flute, clarinet, and bassoon.

In August 1765, the Mozarts finally journeyed homeward but were stalled when both children contracted typhoid fever and remained ill for months. As soon as they were recovered enough to travel, Leopold pressed on. Three and a half years after they left Salzburg, the Mozarts returned home in November 1766.

Compared with cultured cities such as Vienna, Paris, and London, Salzburg appeared drab and rustic to Leopold. It was not the sort of place where Wolfgang could show off his skills and be sufficiently appreciated—or paid well. By the time he turned 12 in 1768, Wolfgang had begun to share his father's low opinion of Salzburg, resenting his post as unpaid concertmaster of the Salzburg court orchestra. Leopold, who made every decision

"Mozart's music is free of all exaggeration, of all sharp breaks and contradictions. The sun shines but does not blind, does not burn or consume. Heaven arches over the earth, but it does not weigh it down, it does not crush or devour it."

— *Karl Barth, influential Swiss theologian*

MITRIDATE
RE DI PONTO,
DRAMMA PER MUSICA
DA RAPPRESENTARSI
NEL REGIO-DUCAL TEATRO
DI MILANO
Nel Carnovale dell' Anno 1771.
DEDICATO
A SUA ALTEZZA SERENISSIMA
IL
DUCA DI MODENA,
REGGIO, MIRANDOLA ec. ec.
AMMINISTRATORE,
E CAPITANO GENERALE
DELLA LOMBARDIA AUSTRIACA
ec. ec.

IN MILANO. )( MDCCLXX.
Nella Stamperia di Giovanni Montani
CON LICENZA DE' SUPERIORI

where Wolfgang's blossoming career was concerned, decided it was time for them to go to Italy so that Wolfgang could try his hand at opera, a form that was sure to test his true mettle as a composer.

Although Wolfgang was not well versed in the style and technique of opera music, he knew what was good—and what was not. As father and son toured the country known as the "birthplace of opera" throughout 1770 and most of 1771, Wolfgang began to hone his musical opinions while he gathered ideas for his first staged opera. *Mitridate, rè di Ponto,* or *Mithridates, King of Pontus* (K. 87), debuted in time for Christmas 1770 in Milan. While not an astounding commercial success, it showed the young composer's grasp of a new technique. Unlike writing symphonic music, writing an opera required a composer to consider

> PERSONAGGI.
>
> MITRIDATE. Rè di Ponto, e d' altri Regni, amante d' Aspasia.
> Sig. Cavaliere Guglielmo D' Ettore Virtuoso di Camera di S. A. S. Elettorale di Baviera.
> ASPASIA, promessa sposa di Mitridate, e già dichiarata Regina,
> Signora Antonia Bernasconi.
> SIFARE, figliuolo di Mitridate, e di Stratonica, amante d' Aspasia,
> Sig. Pietro Benedetti, detto Sartorino.
> FARNACE, primo figliuolo di Mitridate, amante della medesima,
> Sig. Giuseppe Cicognani.
> ISMENE, figlia del Re de' Parti, amante di Farnace,
> Signora Anna Francesca Varese.
> MARZIO, Tribuno Romano, amico di Farnace.
> Sig. Gaspare Bassano.
> ARBATE, Governatore di Ninfea,
> Sig. Pietro Muschietti.
>
> Compositore della Musica.
>
> Il Sig. Cavaliere Amadeo Wolfgango Mozart, Accademico Filarmonico di Bologna, e Maestro della Musica di Camera di S. A. Rma il Principe, ed Arcivescovo di Salisburgo.
>
> ATTO

A page from the program for the first performance of Mitridate describes the characters, called "personaggi" in Italian, involved in the opera

17

the individual singers' voices, along with the story told by the text, when coming up with music that would be entertaining for people to listen to.

When the Mozarts returned to Salzburg in 1772, their new employer, Archbishop Hieronymous Colloredo, started paying Wolfgang for his church music. But Wolfgang saved his best ideas for the music he was not contracted to write. Starting in 1774 with the Symphony No. 29 in A major (K. 201), his pieces began to reflect his passionate and sometimes contrary personality. Wolfgang started making music that he could claim as his own; he was no longer following in others' musical footsteps. But he was still bound to the archbishop and to his father. When he and Leopold were fired in August 1777, though, the 21-year-old was suddenly free to follow his own path. The door had been opened.

olfgang may have been free to go where he pleased, but Leopold was given back his job and required to stay in Salzburg. Not wanting his son to remain in such an antagonistic climate but unable to accompany him himself, the overprotective Leopold decided that his wife should keep an eye on their headstrong son instead. Wolfgang had never been faced with making his own decisions before, and Leopold did not trust his son's ability to effectively manage his own career now. In September 1777, mother and son set out for the southeastern German state of Bavaria, then journeyed farther west to the city of Mannheim. While in Mannheim, Wolfgang fell madly in love with a promising soprano singer named Aloysia Weber, writing several arias specifically for the 15-year-old. Leopold, who was trying to

manage his son's tour from home, did not approve of the distraction the girl presented and ordered Wolfgang to move on to Paris.

In Paris, Anna Maria fell ill and died suddenly in July 1778, and the Mozart family was torn apart. Anna Maria and Leopold's marriage had been a close, happy one, despite the strain of frequent travel and long periods of absence from each other. A bitter Leopold blamed his son for not taking better care of her. Wolfgang sought solace with the Weber family, only to have his heart broken when Aloysia refused to marry him. Determined to keep him in the family, Aloysia's mother soon arranged for Wolfgang to instead marry her third daughter, Constanze. Although Wolfgang was not widely known yet, Constanze

Constanze's older sister Aloysia (pictured) became a well-known soprano singer in Vienna, and Mozart enjoyed writing songs that flattered her voice

could sense his greatness and was eager to marry him. Too eager, Leopold thought.

Against his father's will, Wolfgang spent much of 1780 and 1781 in Vienna and Munich, traveling with the Webers and cultivating relationships with nobles and minor royalty. He traveled to Munich to oversee the production of his opera *Idomeneo, rè di Creta,* or *Idomeneus, King of Crete* (K. 366), which was favorably received when it premiered in January 1781, but its success led to nothing else. Leopold feared that his son was throwing away his life and talent by staying in Vienna with the Webers. For eight months, Leopold refused to give his consent to Wolfgang and Constanze's desire to marry, but the loyal son would not marry without it.

Mozart's 1787 comedic opera about the infamous womanizer Don Juan, called Don Giovanni in Italian, was one of his most brilliant works

"Mozart is the greatest composer of all. Beethoven created his music,

but the music of Mozart is of such purity and beauty that one feels

he merely found it—that it has always existed as part of the inner

beauty of the universe waiting to be revealed."

— Scientist and 20th-century Mozart scholar Albert Einstein

Despite the strained relationship with his father, Wolfgang continued in his daily routine of teaching lessons to Viennese children, composing music, and playing for important people. In July 1781, Wolfgang was commissioned to write a new opera called *Die Entführung aus dem Serail*, or *The Abduction from the Seraglio* (K. 384), and he pursued the project with zest. Every day, "I rush to my desk with the greatest eagerness and remain seated there with the greatest delight," he wrote. One month after the premiere of the successful comic opera, in August 1782, Wolfgang and Constanze wed. The next day, Leopold's written consent arrived in the mail.

The year 1782 was also a pivotal one for Wolfgang's musical development. It was the year he learned about the work of George Frideric Handel and Johann Sebastian Bach, two of the greatest composers of the Baroque era. In Mozart's day, the term "classical music" usually referred to the music of the period between 1600 and 1750, which was characterized by an ornamental style of architecture known as "baroque." Composers such as Handel and Bach took elements from the preceding era of Renaissance music and made music that was more complex and ornamental (like baroque architecture), more emotional, and more difficult to play. Wolfgang built upon the foundations of their forms and techniques and,

with his use of a technique called counterpoint, perfected the "Classical" style that would come to be almost synonymous with the name Mozart.

By his late 20s, Wolfgang had reached the pinnacle of his musical powers, but he was still relatively unknown. He believed he needed to compose something that would showcase all he had to offer. He needed an opera, one that would prove that he deserved an important place in the Viennese court, one that would catapult him into the ranks of the best German composers of his day. In 1785, he would finally get his chance to shine.

As Wolfgang once wrote to his father, "Do not forget how much I desire to write operas. I envy anyone who is composing one. I could really weep for vexation when I hear or see an aria." Wolfgang was desperate to write a successful opera, but he was also looking for another source of income besides teaching lessons and playing concerts. Playing in public was becoming a strain on his small hands, as the pieces he played were usually physically demanding. And since outgrowing his fame as a child prodigy, the mature Wolfgang was not able to draw the crowds that he once had.

By 1785, Wolfgang had grown increasingly frustrated with the musical hierarchy in Vienna that would not allow him to write what he wished; the Viennese court was already dominated by other composers, and, as might be expected, they did not want to make room for him. He felt that other operas of the day were inferior to anything he could compose, and he was simply waiting for an opportunity to present itself. When his friend and well-known librettist Lorenzo Da Ponte approached Wolfgang in October 1785 about collaborating on a new opera, Wolfgang knew precisely upon what play they should base their work. He had read Pierre Beaumarchais' 1784 comedic play *Le Mariage de Figaro* (*The Marriage of Figaro*) and knew the story would be perfect for such an undertaking. Its account of

Mozart (left-most figure in picture) was a member of a secret society called the Freemasons, whose meetings were held in grand temples

one chaotic day in the palace of the Italian Count and Countess Almaviva involved love, intrigue, mistaken identities, and revelations—the kind of story that lent itself well both to the stage and to music.

Before they could begin work in earnest, Wolfgang and Da Ponte first had to secure the approval of Emperor Joseph II, who had banned the original Beaumarchais work from the stages of Vienna because of its satirical tone toward the aristocratic class. Da Ponte translated the play into Italian poetry, excised any objectionable or overtly political material, and created the entire libretto in six weeks. Da Ponte's translation and abridgement of the play inspired Mozart's musical compositions, and together, they produced an incred-

LE NOZZE

DIE HOCHZEI

*Eine comische Oper*

in Musik

*von*

WOLFGANG AMA

ible set of realistic opera characters within an opera buffa frame.

Wolfgang's advancements in counterpoint enabled him to weave together the various strands of musical characterization so seamlessly that the music, the action of the play, and the characters themselves all moved together at the same pace and complemented each other. Wolfgang's passionate characters and musically driven plot took opera to a new level. Nothing in *Figaro* was out of joint. Every note was placed for a purpose, and each melody worked with its harmony. Perhaps because of the adjustments he had to make once they started working with particular singers, Wolfgang did

CLAVIEI

HAM

# DI FIGARO
## DES FIGARO

*n vier Aufzügen*

*setzt*

# *EUS MOZART*

not complete the musical score until April 1786, when *Figaro*'s cast had already begun rehearsing at the theater where the premiere would take place, Vienna's famous Burgtheater.

*Le nozze di Figaro*, or *The Marriage of Figaro* (K. 492), premiered at the Burgtheater on May 1, 1786, with Wolfgang directing the orchestra and singers. The four-hour opera was a triumph for Wolfgang, both personally and professionally, but the success of *Figaro* did not guarantee him sustained employment. In fact, he received no offers from the emperor or any member of Joseph's court following the short run of *Figaro*. Like many

*AUSZUG*

*URG*

operas of the time, *Figaro* did not have a long shelf life; after being presented to enthusiastic, overflowing audiences for nine performances throughout the rest of the year, it was put away to make room for other operas written by lesser composers.

However, months later, while visiting friends in the city of Prague, Wolfgang was delighted to learn that *Figaro* was still a raging success there. The opera's music was being played everywhere, especially within smaller ensembles in people's homes. The arias meant

Austrian composer Franz Schubert was born near Vienna almost six years after Mozart's death and grew to admire his predecessor's talent

29

"A world that has produced a Mozart is a world worth saving.

What a picture of a better world you have given us, Mozart!"

— *Austrian composer Franz Schubert*

for a solo vocalist were being played on piano or wind instruments; the duets and trios usually sung between characters were rewritten for string quartets or clavier duets. Some even interpreted *Figaro* through dance. Inspired by the effect his music was having on people, Wolfgang looked to the future in eager anticipation, certain that this time, he would reach the heights of fame and fortune that he had been seeking all his life.

"In my dreams of heaven, I always see the great Masters gathered in a huge hall in which they all reside. Only Mozart has his own suite."

— *Danish pianist and comedian Victor Borge*

In response to the citizens of Prague's request for an opera, *Don Giovanni* premiered in Vienna the following May of 1788. That year, Wolfgang wrote several smaller pieces in addition to his last three symphonies. The third, Symphony No. 41 in C, later nicknamed the "Jupiter" (K. 551), was never performed during his lifetime, and after he completed that project in August 1788, his level of production decreased significantly. Not until one year later, in August 1789, when *The Marriage of Figaro* was staged for a second time in Vienna, did his mood improve. The pressures of supporting his wife and five-year-old son Karl were gradually draining Wolfgang's emotional and compositional reserves. In addition

to his disappointment at not receiving any new commissions, he was also concerned about Constanze's health during the late 1780s, as she had been ill and suffered the deaths of four babies in seven years. Perhaps worst of all, Wolfgang could not concentrate on the one thing that had always brought him peace—his music.

That music was no longer as well received as it had been up until 1786. For 34-year-old Wolfgang, such negative public sentiment could not have come at a worse time. His professional frustrations only increased his sense of despair. He was self-conscious, no longer as vain about his abilities, and he began to doubt whether life would ever get better. This was not the life he and Constanze had imagined for themselves. His depression suddenly lifted in 1791, though, and Wolfgang's productivity surged. He completed two operas, *La*

Due to the 1789 French Revolution and the years that followed, Mozart was confined to travel within only Austria and Germany for his final three years

33

*clemenza di Tito*, or *The Clemency of Titus* (K. 621), and *Die Zauberflöte*, or *The Magic Flute* (K. 620), several chamber works, and a couple of concertos.

During the summer of 1791, while he was hard at work finishing the operas, Wolfgang was commissioned to write a requiem, or mass for the dead, by Franz Count von Walsegg. The German count's wife had died in February, and he wished to have a piece written in her memory; that he also wished to claim the composition as his own is why he commissioned

Wolfgang anonymously. A messenger was sent to the Mozarts' house, and Wolfgang never dealt with the count in person. Wolfgang and one of his students, 25-year-old Franz Xaver Süssmayer, set to work on the Requiem in D minor (K. 626) in the fall. Although Wolfgang was not feeling well during much of the time he worked on the Requiem, he became obsessive about its completion, sacrificing what was left of his health to devote time to this final and ultimately incomplete work.

Because Mozart (in bed) was too sick to leave his house, the musicians came to him so that he could construct parts of the unfinished Requiem

Only the Requiem's opening, "Requiem aeternum," would be complete at the time of Wolfgang's death, and another pupil and friend would finish the "Kyrie." That left eight parts, which remained in fragments, and five that had nothing begun on them at all. Those 13 parts would be completed by Süssmayer, whose compositional skills were still rudimentary and whose ability was limited at best. Yet keeping him on to finish her husband's commission would be Constanze's only recourse if she wanted to collect the remaining payment from Count von Walsegg.

Even though Mozart was not responsible for the majority of what later became the Requiem, the work would always be attributed to him, and it would always be shrouded

*The last time Mozart performed in public was to conduct a piece he had written for the dedication of his Masonic lodge's new temple in late 1791*

"**Mozart exists, and will exist, eternally; divine Mozart—less a name, more a soul descending to us from the heavens, who appeared on this earth, stayed for a little over thirty years, and left it all the more rejuvenated, richer and happier for his appearance.**"

— *Charles Gounod, 19th-century French composer*

Because the Requiem (a page of which is shown here in Mozart's hand-writing) was left unfinished, later composers added their interpretations

in the shadowy circumstances of his death. Perhaps no other piece of music would be the subject of so many myths, and few composers would ever equal the artistic legacy of the man who envisioned it.

Wolfgang finally succumbed to illness around November 20 and took to bed. By the beginning of December, he was in the throes of a terrible fever. For centuries after his death, Wolfgang would be reputed to have died of various kinds of poisoning, with one of the most popular theories being that rival composer Antonio Salieri had been the agent of his death. But Wolfgang's high fever, projectile vomiting, and swollen hands and feet point

A mid-19th-century work called The Last Hours of Mozart, by Henry Nelson O'Neil, does not show the true agony of Mozart's fatal illness

39

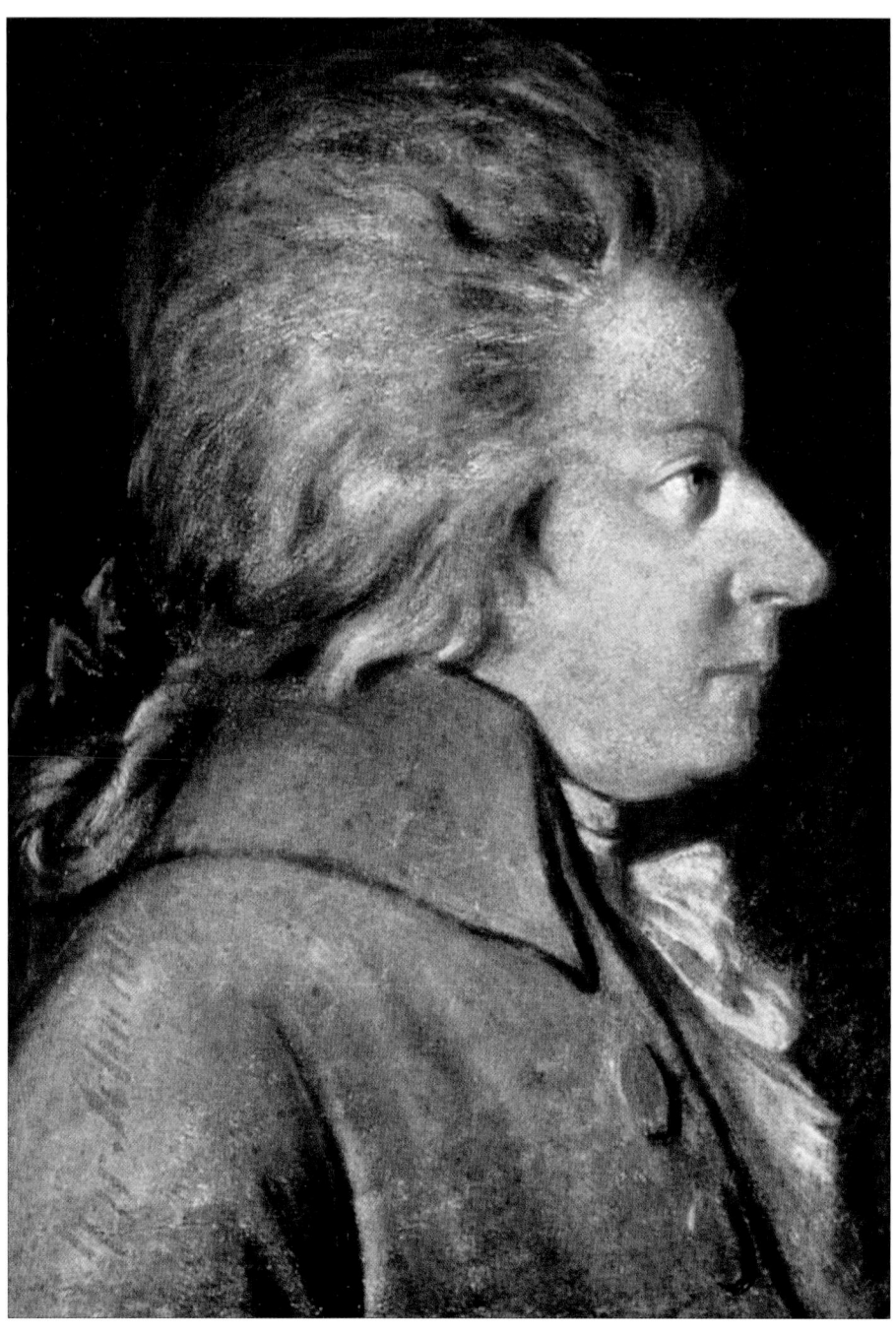

to the inflammatory disease of rheumatic fever as the true cause. Wolfgang died in the early hours of December 5, 1791, and was buried discreetly and privately at Vienna's Saint Mark's Cemetery late the following day. More popular after his death than during his life, Wolfgang Amadeus Mozart would live on through his immortal music.

**"The riddle of Mozart is precisely that 'the man' refuses to be a key for solving it. In death, as in life, he conceals himself behind his work."**

*— German author and Mozart biographer Wolfgang Hildesheimer*

Since Mozart spent the greater part of his life either on the road or far away from family and friends, he wrote many letters. Much of his correspondence survives and has been translated into English and other languages. In the following letter, Mozart thanks a family friend, a young clergyman named Bullinger, for helping his grieving father cope with Anna Maria's death in July 1778. It offers insight into the 22-year-old's low opinions of Salzburg—and high opinions of himself.

*To Abbé Bullinger, Salzburg; Paris, 7 August 1778*

*Dearest Friend!*

*Allow me above all to thank you most warmly for the new proof of friendship you have given me by your kind interest in my dear father—first in preparing him for his loss and then in consoling him so sympathetically. You played your part most admirably—these are my father's own words. Most beloved friend, how can I thank you sufficiently? You have saved my dear father for me; I have you to thank that I still have him. Permit me to say no more on this subject and not to attempt to express my gratitude, for indeed I feel far too weak, too incompetent—too weary to do so. Most beloved friend! I am always your debtor. But patience! On my honor I am not yet in a position to repay what I owe you—but do not doubt me, for God will grant me the opportunity of showing by deeds what I am unable to express in words.... You say that I should now think only of my father and that I should disclose all my thoughts to him with entire frankness and put my trust in him. How unhappy should I be if I needed the reminder! It was expedient that you should suggest it, but I am glad to say (and you will be glad to hear it) that I do not need this advice. In my last letter to my dear father I told him what I myself knew up to the time, assuring him that I should always report everything to him very fully and inform him candidly of my views, because I placed my entire confidence in him and trusted completely to his fatherly care, love, and goodness. I feel sure that some day he will not deny me a request on which the whole happiness and peace of my life depend and which will certainly be quite fair and reasonable, for he cannot expect anything else from me. Dearest friend, do not let my father read this. You know him. He would only worry, and quite unnecessarily.*

*Now for our Salzburg story. You, most beloved friend, are well aware how I detest Salzburg—and not only on account of the injustices which my dear father and I have endured there, which in themselves would be enough to make us wish to forget such a place and blot it out of our memory forever! ... Perhaps you will misunderstand me and think that Salzburg is too small for me? If so, you are greatly mistaken. I have already given some of my reasons to my father. In the meantime, content yourself with this one, that Salzburg is no place for my talent. In the first place, professional musicians there are not held in much consideration; and, secondly, one hears nothing, there is no theater, no opera; and even if they really wanted one, who is there to sing? For the last five or six years the Salzburg orchestra has always been rich in what is useless and superfluous, but very poor in what is necessary, and absolutely destitute of what is indispensable; and such is the case at the present moment....*

Knowing that his father was opposed to his intention to marry Constanze Weber, Mozart wrote the following letter to Leopold, begging him to see things from his point of view. Mozart outlines his rationale for why the present is the perfect time for him to get married, and he paints a candid portrait of his wife-to-be.

*To Leopold Mozart; Vienna, 15 December 1781*

*Dearest father! You demand an explanation of the words in the closing sentence of my last letter! Oh, how gladly would I have opened my heart to you long ago, but I was deterred by the reproaches you might have made to me for thinking of such a thing at an unseasonable time—although indeed thinking can never be unseasonable. Meanwhile I am very anxious to secure here a small but certain income, which, together with what chance may provide, will enable me to live here quite comfortably—and then—to marry! You are horrified at the idea? But I entreat you, dearest, most beloved father, to listen to me. I have been obliged to reveal my intentions to you. You must, therefore, allow me to disclose to you my reasons, which moreover, are very well founded. The voice of nature speaks as loud in me as in others, louder, perhaps, than in many a big strong lout of a fellow. I simply cannot live as most young men do in these days. In the first place, I have too much religion; in the second place, I have too great a love of my neighbor and too high a feeling of honor to seduce an innocent girl; and, in the third place, I have too much horror and disgust, too much dread and fear of diseases and too much care for my health to fool about with women.... But owing to my disposition, which is more inclined to a peaceful and domesticated existence than to revelry, I who from my youth up have never been accustomed to look after my own belongings, linen, clothes and so forth, cannot think of anything more necessary to me than a wife. I assure you that I am often obliged to spend unnecessarily, simply because I do not pay attention to things. I am absolutely convinced that I should manage better with a wife (on the same income which I have now) than I do by myself. And how many useless expenses would be avoided! True, other expenses would have to be met, but—one knows what they are and can be prepared for them—in short, one leads a well-ordered existence. A bachelor, in my opinion, is only half alive. Such are my views and I cannot help it. I have thought the matter over and reflected sufficiently, and I shall not change my mind. But who is the object of my love? Do not be horrified again, I entreat you. Surely not one of the Webers? Yes, one of the Webers—but not Josefa, nor Sophia, but Constanze, the middle one. In no other family have I ever come across such differences of character. The eldest is a lazy, gross, perfidious woman,* and as cunning as a fox. Mme. Lange [Aloysia] is a false, malicious person and a coquette. The youngest is still too young to be anything in particular—she is just a good-natured, but feather-headed creature! May God protect her from seduction! But the middle one, my good, dear Constanze, is the martyr of the family, and, probably for that very reason, is the kindest-hearted, the cleverest and in short, the best of them all. She makes herself responsible for the whole household and yet in their opinion she does nothing right. Oh, my most beloved father, I could fill whole sheets with descriptions of all the scenes that I have witnessed in that house. If you want to read them, I shall do so in my next letter. But before I cease to plague you with my chatter, I must make you better acquainted with the character of my dear Constanze. She is not ugly, but at the same time far from beautiful. Her whole beauty consists in two little black eyes and a pretty figure. She has no wit, but she has enough common sense to enable her to fulfill her duties as a wife and mother. It is a downright lie that she is inclined to be extravagant. On the contrary, she is accustomed to be shabbily dressed, for the little that her mother has been able to do for her children, she has done for the two others, but never for Constanze. True, she would like to be neatly and cleanly dressed, but not smartly, and most things that a woman needs she is able to make for herself; and she dresses her own hair every day. Moreover, she understands housekeeping and has the kindest heart in the world. I love her and she loves me with all her heart. Tell me whether I could wish myself a better wife? One thing more I must tell you, which is that when I resigned the Archbishop's service, our love had not yet begun. It was born of her tender care and attentions when I was living in their house.

Up until his marriage to Constanze, Mozart wrote to his sister Nannerl regularly. Like her father, Nannerl did not approve of Constanze, and in this letter, Mozart entreats his sister to respond kindly to his future wife's attempt at getting to know her. Mozart also provides glimpses into his compositional process and expert musical interpretation by describing a piece he has written for Nannerl to play on the clavier.

*To Nannerl; Vienna, 20 April 1782*

*Dearest Sister!*
*My dear Constanze has at last summoned up courage to follow the impulse of her kind heart—that is, to write to you, my dear sister! Should you be willing to favor her with a reply (and indeed I hope you will, so that I may see the sweet creature's delight reflected on her face), may I beg you to enclose your letter to me? I only mention this as a precaution and so that you may know that her mother and sisters are not aware that she has written to you....*

*The reason why I did not reply to your letter at once was that on account of the wearisome labor of writing these small notes, I could not finish the composition any sooner. And, even so, it is awkwardly done, for the prelude ought to come first and the fugue to follow. But I composed the fugue first and wrote it down while I was thinking out the prelude. I only hope that you will be able to read it, for it is written so very small; and I hope further that you will like it. Another time I shall send you something better for the clavier. My dear Constanze is really the cause of this fugue's coming into the world. Baron von Swieten, to whom I go every Sunday, gave me all the works of Handel and Sebastian Bach to take home with me (after I had played them to him). When Constanze heard the fugues, she absolutely fell in love with them. Now she will listen to nothing but fugues, and particularly (in this kind of composition) the works of Handel and Bach. Well, as she had often heard me play fugues out of my head, she asked me if I had ever written any down, and when I said I had not, she scolded me roundly for not recording some of my compositions in this most artistic and beautiful of all musical forms and never ceased to entreat me until I wrote down a fugue for her. So this is its origin. I have purposely written above it* Andante maestoso, *as it must not be played too fast. For if a fugue is not played slowly, the ear cannot clearly distinguish the theme when it comes in and consequently the effect is entirely missed.*

**1756**

*Wolfgang Amadeus Mozart is born in Salzburg, Austria, on January 27.*

**1760**

*Leopold Mozart begins teaching Wolfgang how to play the clavier and the violin.*

**1762–1763**

*Mozart takes his first tour abroad and performs before Emperor Francis I and Empress Maria Theresa of Germany.*

**1764**

*Mozart meets renowned composer Johann Christian Bach, son of Johann Sebastian Bach, while touring England.*

**1766**

*The first public performance of one of Mozart's symphonies (K. 22) occurs in Amsterdam, the Netherlands.*

**1770**

*While in Rome, Mozart and Leopold attend a service at the Sistine Chapel, then meet Pope Clement XIV.*

**1774**

*Mozart composes* La finta giardiniera, *or* The Phony Gardener *(K. 196), his second comic opera.*

**1777**

*Archbishop Hieronymous Colloredo fires the Mozarts when they request leave to take another tour; Wolfgang begins touring Germany and France.*

**1778**

*Anna Maria dies in Paris; Leopold blames Mozart, and a rift develops between father and son.*

**1780**

*With his opera* Idomeneo, *Mozart challenges the conventions of opera and develops a new style.*

**1782**

*Mozart marries Constanze Weber on August 4; of their six children, only two will see adulthood.*

**1782–1785**

*Mozart composes six volumes of string quartets, dedicating them to fellow composer Franz Joseph Haydn.*

**1786**

The Marriage of Figaro, *one of Mozart's most enduring operas, is performed for the first time in Vienna.*

**1787**

*Sixteen-year-old Ludwig van Beethoven comes to Vienna in April to study with Mozart.*

**1788**

*Mozart composes his last symphony, No. 41 in C (K. 551), the "Jupiter."*

**1791**

*Mozart dies on December 5 in Vienna.*

archbishop — *The head of the Catholic Church who is responsible for the Catholics living in a particular district; in Mozart's day, Salzburg (then part of Germany) was controlled politically and religiously by the archbishop*

aria — *A long solo for an opera singer, usually accompanied by a few instruments, that allows the action of the opera to slow down and focus on one particular moment and one individual character's situation*

Bach, Johann Sebastian — *A prolific composer and talented organist from Germany, Bach helped shape the course of music during the Baroque period; his pieces are known for their depth and technicality as well as their artistry*

Classical music — *In the strictest sense, the Classical period lasted from about 1730 to 1820 and is characterized by clean, well-structured music that has clear melodies and a range of emotional coloring*

clavier — *An instrument with a keyboard that served as the precursor to the present-day piano; 18th-century claviers, also known as harpsichords, had strings that the keys on the keyboard plucked inside the wooden case*

concertmaster — *The principal violinist in an orchestra; this person is considered to be the orchestra's instrumental leader as well, second in command only to the conductor*

counterpoint — *The relationship between two or more independent voices that share a harmony but seem to move in opposite directions; Classical composers used counterpoint to more clearly define the melodies and harmonies present in their works*

Habsburg Empire — *Austria and lands throughout Eastern Europe (also including Spain, parts of France and Italy, and the Netherlands) that were ruled by monarchs from a family line known as Habsburg from the 13th century until 1918*

Handel, George Frideric — *A German-born composer who spent most of his life in England; his influential works helped music transition from the Baroque to the Classical period*

libretto — *The text of an opera, which is usually written by someone other than the composer of the opera's music; a librettist is the person who writes the text*

opera buffa — *A genre of comic opera that is sung in Italian and often based on real-life characters; it developed in Naples, Italy, in the early 18th century as a contrasting style to opera seria, or tragic opera*

Renaissance music — *Music written in Europe during the Renaissance (c. 1400–1600) and used commonly for church services (such as masses) or secular purposes (such as the madrigal form, songs sung for entertainment)*

Blom, Eric, ed. *Mozart's Letters.* Baltimore: Penguin Books Inc., 1961.

Boerner, Steve. "Biography." The Mozart Project. http://www.mozartproject.org/biography/index.html.

Davenport, Marcia. *Mozart.* New York: Dorset Press, 1960.

Gutman, Robert W. *Mozart: A Cultural Biography.* New York: Harcourt Brace, 1999.

Rushton, Julian. *Mozart.* Oxford: Oxford University Press, 2006.

Solomon, Maynard. *Mozart: A Life.* New York: HarperCollins, 1995.

Steinberg, Michael. *Choral Masterworks: A Listener's Guide.* New York: Oxford University Press, 2005.